—THE— PAIN IN HER EYES

WHY MENTAL HEALTH SHOULD NEVER BE OVERLOOKED

The Pain In Her Eyes

Why Mental Health Should Never Be Overlooked

For permission requests, please contact the author at **caitlincummins@gmail.com**

First Edition: June 2026

ISBN: 979-8-9955287-3-9 (Hardcover)

ISBN: 979-8-9955287-1-5 (Paperback)

ISBN: 979-8-9955287-4-6 (ebook)

Library of Congress Control Number: 2026908465

Printed in the United States of America

Content Warning

Please be advised that this book contains detailed and real-life depictions of **domestic violence, physical assault, self-harm, suicidal ideation,** and other **graphic content.** These themes are central to the story's exploration of mental health in this generation.

Reader discretion is strongly advised. Please prioritize your well-being as you read.

If you or someone you know is in need of support, please contact a local crisis resource or the **988 Suicide & Crisis Lifeline** (in the US).

International: Please contact your local emergency services.

To my family and the Webers

Thank you for loving me before I had the words to tell you why I was hurting.

CONTENTS

A Note from the Author

Dear reader,

Thank you for choosing to open this book.

Writing ***The Pain In Her Eyes*** was a journey through the darkest corners of my own life. This is a story born from a desire to speak the realities that are so often whispered in the shadows or kept behind closed doors. Many in our generation have been told to keep moving without acknowledging the crushing weight of what we are holding back.

I wrote this book for the people who feel unseen and unheard, for those who have fought in silence, and for anyone trying to navigate the heavy complexities of trauma in our modern world. While the realities ahead are real, raw, and, at times, difficult to read, I hope that by sharing my own story, I can offer you a sense of resonance. I want this to be a reminder that your story matters, your pain is valid, and no one has to walk through the fire alone.

Please remember: Because these events are real, they may feel more intense as you read. If at any point the narrative feels like too much, please listen to your heart. Put the book down. Breathe. Walk away for as long as you need. Your peace of mind is far more important than finishing a chapter.

Thank you for trusting me with your time and for having the courage to look at the hard realities of the world with me.

Much love,

caitlincummins

Introduction

System Initialization

They say the eyes are a window to the soul, but mine were a door locked against a world that wasn't ready for the story I had yet to tell. So much of our lives is spent perfecting the "outside"—polishing the surface and making sure the world sees a version of us that is "fine." Behind that shut door, there was a chaos I didn't yet have the words to name.

For a long time, I believed that if I kept moving fast enough, the noise would dissipate. You become an expert at the performance, a master of the "I'm okay," while the internal pressure builds until the hinges start to scream. I chose to share my story now, not because it's easy, but because it's necessary. We live in a society that often treats mental health like a secret we're supposed to keep—a "check engine" light we're told to ignore.

We're taught to silence it, but silence is not a fix; it's a delay. If mental health is an afterthought, so is the quality of our life. I wanted to share my story to help others, hoping my experiences offer encouragement to anyone who has felt the same. Whether you are currently staring at a flickering dashboard or you've been parked in the dark for too long, know that your story holds a purpose the world is ready to hear.

Chapter 1

Source Code

My life didn't just start; it was placed into the hands of the people who would become my entire world. I was born on June 16, 2005, into the most loving family I could have dreamt of. My family is the reason I am who I am, and I wouldn't change it for anything. I live with the humbling realization that I am the luckiest girl in the world—that God looked at this specific, intentional circle and chose me to be part of it.

I have one brother, Jake, one sister, Kylie, two Golden Retrievers, a Maltese, and the most loving parents. Together, they have given me the most amazing life imaginable, which I could never thank them enough for. They were the architects of a childhood that felt like a masterpiece. I'm in awe of the colors they chose to paint my life with.

I often say I owe them everything, not just for the roof over my head, but for the profound way they curated our world. The intentionality of moments that I only fully appreciated as I got older, and the love that never stopped, made us who we are. My parents are so purposeful in everything they do, carrying that same warmth and care into every interaction they have with others.

I grew up in Southern California, in a house where I have the best memories. I would give anything to relive those moments in real time rather than just in my mind, but

I am so grateful to have a family that prioritized creating them, because not everyone can say that.

My family got the keys to Hathaway on my due date—it felt hardcoded into my existence from the first update. We lived at Hathaway for thirteen years—the home we brought Chloe, Cooper, and Whitney to for the first time.

If you closed your eyes and asked me to describe "childhood," I wouldn't show you a photo; I'd show you that house. I'd show you the specific sunlight that hit the floor where Chloe, Cooper, and Whitney first learned to trust us. Lastly, I'd show you the hallway where Kylie broke her foot while filming a "dog vlog" before we moved, which is on camera, by the way.

It was the kind of home you could break a foot and have no regrets. Not only was Hathaway pure gold, but the neighborhood was filled with the most incredible people. That home was the backdrop of every "first"—the place where the entirety of my childhood was written and dried.

Saturday mornings were when the sound of our Goldens barking acted as an alarm to wake up for breakfast. I can still see the flour dusting the counter and the way my siblings and I would navigate the "obstacle course" of dogs weaving between our feet. Our Goldens were always underfoot, waiting for anything to hit the ground.

Our home was powered by the love and affection of our family. It was loud, it was chaotic, and it was the kind of perfect I didn't realize I'd one day wish to relive.

When you're young, all you think about is what life is like when you're older. When that time comes, all you think about is how you felt when you didn’t know how cruel the world was.

I spent so much time imagining the girl I would become that I forgot to appreciate the girl I was: the one who didn't yet know what it felt like to have the world go quiet.

In February 2019, we turned the page to a new chapter, moving to a second, gorgeous property just twenty minutes away. Its open layout was a soundstage designed for hosting—a vast space waiting for the laughter of the crowd we were supposed to have.

Prior to stepping onto the threshold of starting high school, the world abruptly shifted in a direction no one could have predicted. A global pandemic erased the horizon of my freshman year, reducing the vibrant, chaotic world I had anticipated to the cold “dimension” of a laptop screen.

The silence of 2020 turned our home into an empty set—a hollow echo waiting for an audience that was no longer allowed to arrive. Spending that entire first semester in digital isolation was a theft of life events I had spent my childhood looking forward to. Everything was systematically canceled. Socializing had become a legal liability. The world had shifted on its axis, and everything changed.

Every fun, exciting thing high school offers was scrubbed from the plans. The brightness that filled the idea of high school had been shadowed by darkness—not a sudden power outage, but a slow degradation of the “best years” I had spent my childhood writing.

The dream of hearing the sound of a full football stadium on Friday nights was replaced with a deafening silence where you could hear every thought that crossed your mind.

My camera roll was supposed to be full—an archive full of football games, homecoming, crowded hallways, and stupid activities teenagers partake in. Instead, it remained empty, a series of blank thumbnails where my life was supposed to be recorded. Every memory that "should have" existed didn't.

The gravity of everyone's life had been recalibrated overnight. This home became the place where my internal world had to grow because my external world had been forced to stop. We had moved into this home with the intention of filling it with people. It was a "host's dream," with a backyard that felt like a private resort.

We were once the house where cars lined the curb every weekend, and the kitchen island was always covered in snacks for friends. Suddenly, Saturday mornings lost their "reward" status.

When every day is spent inside with the rest of your life on pause, the weekend feels less like a getaway and more like a continuation of the same intermission.

There is a haunting stillness from sitting in a house that feels like a vacation, yet your world feels like it's in a waiting room. I was staring at a door that I couldn't open, anticipating a life I wasn't allowed to start.

I would often lie out under the sun, letting the heat press against my skin, trying to feel something—anything that didn't involve a Wi-Fi connection or a digital restriction.

I was a fifteen-year-old girl trying to absorb enough warmth to offset the coldness of isolation. I would close my eyes and hear the electric roar of a stadium, the collective surge of the crowd, and the buttery salt of popcorn. But when I opened them, it had all been stripped. An experience no one was allowed to live.

Chapter 2

Air Gapped

When January 2021 came, they gave us the "option" to return to campus. I took it, not because the environment felt safe, but because I was desperate to initialize some version of a real high school experience. I needed a System Restore. But "in-person" was a simulation.

We were masked, distanced, and muted—restricted by the code of "Social Distancing"—the hallways, which should have been high-octane social hubs, felt like sterilized server rooms. We were physically present, but the Connection Status remained "NOT FOUND."

The most terrifying part of the "Safety Protocol" was the Security Vulnerabilities. To keep the air circulating, classroom doors were completely open at all times. On an open-access campus where anyone could walk in, those open doors felt like unsecured access points—an imminent breach waiting to happen.

I was sitting in a classroom trying to do everything right while my internal Threat Detection System was screaming at 100% capacity. The fear wasn't a malfunction; it was a response to the likelihood. We are a generation watching shootings happen on a loop, making every open door feel like a countdown.

Very often, school shootings were highly realistic nightmares I couldn’t run from. These weren't just dreams; they were System Crashes where the sound wasn’t muted, and the impact felt real.

By August 2021, the “update” finally arrived. Everyone was back. Football games, homecoming, the high-octane social scenes I’d waited my entire life for—it all felt surreal. For a moment, it seemed like the System was overclocking to make up for the lost year. I wanted to believe that the Source Code of my life was being rewritten into something new.

But by November, the excitement hit a Terminal System Error. The depression didn't arrive with a warning; it was a background process. I’d show up to class feeling entirely degraded, wondering why I’d ever fought so hard to be in a place that felt so hollow. The dream had died.

I initiated a Manual Override. I finished high school at a private, Christian online school in April 2023. It took a long time to admit that the thing I had waited my entire life for was the thing that broke me.

Chapter 3 | Error 404

Road Not Found

[Status: Error 404: Road Not Found]

The general concept of turning sixteen is sold to us as a cinematic montage. A gift-wrapped key, a “voilà” moment, a girl pulls out of the driveway, the wind catches her hair, and the credits roll.

After spending my fifteenth year in a digital waiting room, staring at a door I couldn't open, sixteen was supposed to be the “system update.” Instead, the update was jammed. I was staring at a loading circle that was working tirelessly to give me absolutely nothing.

This summer was one long, lagging signal that kept generating Error Codes. It was a high-latency existence where my intentions never matched reality.

I would take a test, but the System would lag. By the time the command reached the world, the signal was corrupted. My first driver’s test was June 17, 2021—the day after my sixteenth birthday. There is a specific kind of tactical math involved in that scheduling.

Obviously, you wait a day. You don’t gamble with the emotional sanctity of your birthday. If by some tragic intent the world wants you to fail, you should at least have twenty-four hours to enjoy the "Sixteen" rebrand before it is systematically dismantled.

On June 16th, I was a girl of pure potential. For those twenty-four hours, I was legally sixteen, which meant I was theoretically free. June 17th arrived with a clinical, grey light.

The waiting room I had experienced at home didn't disappear. It traded spaces for the beige purgatory of the Department of Motor Vehicles—an address change that felt like a server room. It felt cold, empty, and regardless of the time put into the process, progress stayed at zero percent.

I wasn't a girl with a birthday anymore; I was a sequence of data points waiting to be verified. There was a gut feeling, a System Warning I wanted to pretend didn't exist.

I was a girl trying to outrun a corrupted file, praying that if I moved fast enough, the System wouldn't notice the Error. I was trying to avoid the crash, hoping it was a one-and-done scenario.

Try telling that to me, Five Tests Later.

June 17th was a total System Failure. My first driver's test had a lifespan of nine seconds—the shortest distance between "Pure Potential" and "Hardware Error" I had ever traveled.

While pulling out of the parking lot, the back right tire clipped the curb, a jarring glitch in a sequence that should have been seamless.

Time didn't just stop; it lagged. The loading pages went black. There was already an initiated reset; the "address change" I had hoped for was just a return to the original file.

Hardware Failure: System Shutdown

By now, the "Waiting Room" feeling from Chapter One had followed me to the DMV. I had already failed once. I was exhausted by the process, the beige walls, and the pressure of wanting to leave.

I took the second test. I made it out of the parking lot, but halfway through, I committed a "Critical Error," which is a death sentence in the world of the DMV. It doesn't matter if you were 99% perfect; if you miss one blind spot or hesitate at a four-way stop, the cold reality settles in: Automatic Fail.

Two weeks later: Test Number Three. This is where the comedy and the world turned dark—literally. It was pouring, an Atmospheric Glitch that blurred the lines of the road. If you fail your third driver's test, you have to retake your permit test before taking a second set of driver's tests.

Mind you, I had passed my permit test on my first try six months earlier. So all I blame is myself and driver's tests. That hour at the DMV felt like a fever dream. I walked from the car—having failed—directly to the online test. In the span of sixty minutes, I had failed both. No wonder it was pouring and the world was dark.

Error 401: Unauthorized

Taking Test Number Four felt as though the old ones were slowly strangling me. The "Hardware Error" of the curb and the "Atmospheric Glitch" of the rain were still running in the background of my mind.

This was the test I took with a broken finger and two that were sprained from an accident a couple of days prior. The steering wheel became a piece of incompatible hardware—a heavy, rotating reminder that my physical system was currently as broken as the driving record I was trying to fix.

It felt like I was functioning on damaged hardware. It should not be a shock that this test ended with a critical error, along with my first, second, and third. Lucky for you guys, this was the last time.

System Recovery: Manual Override

I was so tired of the process that I preferred high school over driver's tests. To compare, high school felt like a vacation, and the DMV felt like a corrupted destination—one I never wanted to return to.

That being said, Test Number Five was perfect—zero errors. Papers printed, my license existed after three months of grueling retakes and dread.

Having spent so much time at this location, for progress to stay static, it was the first time a sense of completeness existed. The loading circle had reached 100%, and for the first time since the world shifted, a new door unlocked.

Chapter 4

Intentional Damage

Have you ever felt it? That terrifying realization that the exact difference between your family's survival and genuine harm comes down to a sentence you choose to say.

We tend to romanticize the idea of a teenager sneaking out—the open window, the rush of rebellion, the thrill of escape. That wasn't my story. I was a sixteen-year-old girl, agonizing over a response, knowing that saying "no" could bring immediate harm to my family.

My midnight departure was not a reckless "Jailbreak." It was a forced trigger to keep them safe.

I didn't sneak out for a boy because I wanted to. I snuck out because I was terrified of the cost of saying "no." I had seen this movie too many times. The way the repercussions target the girl, and then, inevitably, her family.

The realization of his potential reaction was louder than my own wish to stay safe. It was days before Christmas in 2021—the world was wrapped in the illusion of "peace on earth," while I was calculating the cost of a "no." I broke my own rules so no one had to star in a horror film.

An unauthorized detour

If this next section feels like a sudden detour, it is. To understand the chaotic integration of the family I was born into, let's take a look at family vacations. So, instead of explaining them... how about you live them?

Chapter 5

Dangerous Waters

Ever go on a family vacation and end up with no air at the bottom of the ocean? Your answer should be No. Mine is not. Maui, Hawaii, 2018, was one of the best vacations of my life: such an amazing island and so many memories.

The excursions we booked were amazing—which is our cover word for dangerous. Ziplining hundreds of feet above forests, cliff jumping, and scuba diving. Just to make this clear, we were not clueless. The fact that a potentially dire situation had a perfect ending proves we knew what we were doing.

The risk of catastrophe is always there, and you have to accept that. Otherwise, you are placing all your luck into an expedition that has no perfect safety rate.

As every day is, it was a gorgeous day in Hawaii, and we spent time in a large pool for scuba training before heading out. The water was so clear, a dark crystal blue you could only imagine. It all felt like a movie, but we all know how quickly that changes.

After we descended, we were diving in a very secluded part of the ocean. My dad was swimming in front of me, and I was directly behind him. The rest of my family was ahead of us, so he and I were the only two people who knew what the stakes were in real time.

He accidentally kicked the regulator out of my mouth—your oxygen. The one thing you cannot do is immediately resurface. It does not matter if you ascend slowly; you have to take a five-minute safety stop.

I'm going to be so honest: I felt it leave my mouth, and I felt nothing but calmness. I literally thought, *oh well.* I knew everything would be okay. Even with the stakes being what they were, I still only felt peace. You can't panic, but it really wasn't scary.

Not to me, at least. We both knew exactly what to do, which is how everything worked out. The movie was only rated R for two minutes, then it was back to paradise. The moment itself did not feel nightmare-ish, but the danger associated with freaking out and making the wrong decision absolutely is.

Once we secured the regulator and reset the scene, a second, equally, if not much more serious survival instinct kicked in. We looked at each other and formed an immediate, unspoken pact that echoed through the ocean floor: Do Not Tell Mom.

She was just ahead of us, completely oblivious to the fact that her husband had just accidentally uninstalled her favorite daughter's oxygen supply. He wasn't looking at me like I had almost died; he was looking at me like he was about to die. I was thirteen. He was screwed.

We finished the dive as if it were perfect. I can only imagine my dad was mentally reviewing his life insurance policy. We specifically waited until we were safely on dry land—and preferably in public where she couldn't legally end him—before we casually dropped the truth. Her reaction validated our silence entirely.

Chapter 6

Unauthorized Altitude

Most mid-air emergencies are accidents. Ours was scheduled. Very few people can say they've been handed 100% control of an aircraft with absolutely zero experience, but this wasn't a commercial flight gone wrong. This was Las Vegas, 2022—pure, self-inflicted chaos.

We were each assigned our own plane. An unauthorized, highly unqualified family unit taking over the Nevada airspace. To be fair, there was an actual, licensed pilot sitting in the cockpit with us. Once we hit cruising altitude, the controls were handed over. I was seventeen.

We weren't flying straight and level; we were banking hard. I am talking about executing sharp, aggressive turns so close to the jagged Las Vegas mountains that I could practically count the rocks on the cliff face. One slight twitch of my wrist and my "unauthorized altitude" would have permanently intersected with a wall of solid granite.

Plunging an aircraft into a deliberate, stomach-dropping spin was one of the best experiences ever. The horizon tilted violently. It was a deadly, adrenaline-fueled plummet. When I say deadly—I was actually good at this, hence why I'm alive—but from an outside perspective, "deadly" is the only correct term.

The most terrifying part of this ordeal was knowing that just a few miles away, the rest of my family was executing the same lethal maneuvers at the same time. Somewhere out there, my parents and siblings were also barrel-rolling toward the desert floor.

If anyone at Air Traffic Control had fully grasped that the Cummins family was currently running a synchronized aerial stunt show with absolutely zero credentials, they would have grounded every commercial flight in the Western Hemisphere.

I have no idea how we never got arrested for this. It was legal. Interpret that how you want.

Chapter 7 | Expansion Pack

The Webers

A second family—not by blood, but by a high-speed connection of love. The Webers are the kind of family you dream of growing up with. They have been part of my life since before I took my first breath—growing up at Forest Home, traveling the world, and documenting the kind of "insane" moments that are memories to keep forever.

And by "memories to keep forever," I entirely mean running from the police. You can interpret that how you wish.

Whether we were traversing the streets of Amsterdam in 2025 or navigating the unpredictable chaos of life, our families have always been tethered. We weren't just two families on vacation; we were an Expanded System of siblings and parents who processed every milestone and incident together.

Referencing Chapter Three, they were part of every driver's test I took. When we were on vacation, we had the best time messing with it. Every game referenced the number I had failed at that time. Other than my family, they were the ones who got me through it.

From the unfiltered moments that felt like high-octane movie scenes to the quiet, mundane Friday nights, we never ended up leaving their house. Actually, calling them "quiet" is a lie. Every Friday night we spent there was a complete bypass of any social firewall. It was catastrophic, chaotic, hyper, loud—the kind of laughter that doesn't just make your stomach hurt, it recalibrates your entire soul.

In those moments, the world felt wide open—a high-definition experience shared with the only people who know the "Source Code" of my happiest versions.

Whether we were laughing through the cobblestone streets of Europe or trying not to get arrested, the incidents our families created are ones for the history books. And when I say our families, I entirely mean mine.

We are completely unhinged with each other. There is no filter and, more importantly, no "mute" button.

My family tortures them, so I don't know how they still trust us; I'm genuinely shocked they haven't changed the locks. When I say my family, I'm strictly referring to everyone but me.

If we had a reality show, the season finale would end with all of us sitting in jail. Honestly, it's a Statistical Miracle none of us have been. You know, that's also a lie.

My mom was the culprit; thanks to an unintentional packing error, she almost sent my dad to jail. She packed pocket knives shaped like grenades and guns.

Not to mention, he was flying, and she was driving across the country with us three kids. Seemed very suspicious to the authorities. It was an ordeal, to say the least. The rest of us, however, have stayed far away from that type of closeness.

Even without the TSA threats, our insanity is enough to get us banned from most public places. The parents are just as bad as the rest of us—I take that back, they are so much worse.

There's a specific kind of volume that only occurs when two families are so intertwined that we feel related. You can't tell where one family ends, and the other begins. Fine, that is a lie—none of us look alike—but we act like we were compiled from the same chaotic server.

The Idaho trip of 2021 was a total Hardware Failure. It ended in a complete System Crash—broken bones, sprains, and a lot of pain—but who cares? Clearly not us. In our world, the experience always outpaces the error codes.

The lake decided to render as a solid wall of concrete after we hit a huge pocket of water at high speeds while tubing. That left me with one broken finger, two sprains, and a loss of seven acrylic nails (so heartbreaking) before I even realized I'd hit the surface.

We walked away with a catastrophic damage report, but we also walked away with a story for the family vault. In true Weber-Cummins fashion, the tragedy was immediately archived as a high-priority memory, hard-coded into our family's chaotic legacy.

That break couldn't have healed properly. The pain was a constant high-frequency signal that only silenced when I forced pressure in the opposite direction—a Manual Override.

For three months, the only relief was to make the damage worse, applying pressure so I could steal five seconds of breath.

But that's the thing about being with your favorite people: they take a System Failure and rewrite the file into a story you laugh about, transforming an unpredictable situation into a memory you get to keep.

WEBER-CUMMINS SURVIVAL GUIDE SAFETY WARNING & USER MANUAL

Document Ref: WC-CHAOS-2026-A

Classification: High-Octane Unfiltered Data

Subject: Operational Risks of Multi-Family Synchronization

1. NETWORK ARCHITECTURE (THE CONNECTION) The Weber-Cummins alliance operates on a high-speed connection of love. The System acts as an expanded unit of siblings and parents who process every milestone and incident together. It is a "Logic Error" to try to find where one family ends, and the other begins, as both act as if they were compiled from the same chaotic server.

2. HARDWARE VULNERABILITIES (PHYSICAL DAMAGE) Participation in vacation protocols carries a high risk of hardware failure:

- **The Idaho Tubing Glitch (2021):** A pocket of water may render as solid concrete, resulting in broken bones, sprains, and the loss of seven acrylic nails.
- **Gravity Stress Tests:** Sudden urges to jump out of planes at 13,000 feet are considered "adrenaline rushes."

3. CUSTOMS & BORDER PROTECTION GLITCHES (PARENTAL ERRORS) Parental units may trigger Security Alerts:

- **Packing Errors:** Maternal units may unintentionally pack hardware shaped like grenades and guns, risking the immediate incarceration of paternal units.
- **Legal Miracle Status:** It is a Statistical Miracle that the System has avoided mass arrest thus far.

4. FIREWALL DISCLOSURES (SOCIAL INTERACTION) Friday Night Bypasses: Gatherings at the Weber Residence involve a complete bypass of all social firewalls.

- **Audio Levels:** This System has no "mute" button; expect high-decibel laughter.
- **The "Source Code" Rule:** These individuals are authorized to "torture" you regarding System Errors because they know your happiest versions.

5. EMERGENCY SHUTDOWN There is no "Force Quit" option once an event has been initiated. In a System Crash, the only recovery protocol is to archive the error into a story for the family vault.

USER DISCRETION IS ADVISED.

THE QUICK-START SAFETY CHECKLIST

1.0 Manual Override Required: If a Cummins or a Weber suggests an activity involving "altitude," "velocity," or "water," proceed with Extreme Caution keeping "Catastrophic Event" at a ***99.99% guarantee*** in the back of your mind at all times.

2.0 Hardware Fragility: While broken bones are categorized as a "minor error," the loss of acrylic nails is a **Level 1 Critical Failure.** Mourning periods are Mandatory. Losing seven felt like **death.**

3.0 Restricted Peripherals: Always cross-reference parental luggage before crossing international borders. Maternal units may unintentionally pack pocket knives shaped like grenades and guns, which can result in the immediate (and highly inconvenient) incarceration of paternal units.

4.0 Encrypted Communication: If you see two families communicating via intense eye contact while being hunted by international police, do not intervene. The family unit is self-correcting.

5.0 Data Backup: Every near-death experience must be immediately archived and converted into a "story for the vault." If it was not recorded, did it happen?

End of unauthorized detour

Loading Chapter 8: Initial Deployment

Chapter 8

Initial Deployment

The summer before I left for college was a long-awaited System Restore. For the first time in three years, the "high-frequency" pain of high school finally dissipated, and my resource use dropped to zero.

I spent those months in a reset cycle—packing, laughing, and prepping for a Regional Server Migration that would move my entire life from the California coast to the Arizona desert.

Turning eighteen, the morning after graduating high school a year early, was an adrenaline rush. I dragged my entire family to jump out of a plane. That 13,000-foot Gravity Stress Test was the only time Free-Falling felt like a choice.

The final twenty-four hours on my home server felt surreal. It was strange to realize I had finished an era that was about to be archived forever.

I had spent eighteen years building the excitement for college, but after the pandemic corrupted high school, I couldn't shake the skepticism. College was the dream I'd wanted since I was a little girl, but as the launch date approached, the fear of a System-wide Failure became impossible to ignore.

High school was in the rearview mirror—but somewhere during the drive, the System began to throw Silent Errors. Something felt—corrupted. It felt like a Fatal Error was about to derail the Fresh Start.

I was eighteen years old, staring at the gates of my future, completely unaware that the "Fresh Start" I'd prayed for was a countdown to a total Override.

Misinterpreting the silence for safety, the System was Redlining in the background, and my "Fresh Start" was less than twenty-four hours away from a total impact that no amount of prep work could have prevented.

Chapter 9

Fatal Exception

[Event Log: 14:02:12]

The countdown hit zero exactly twenty-four hours after the Fresh Start had initiated. It wasn't just an accident; it was a Fatal Exception that triggered a catastrophic crash.

I was the variable that caused the accident. No one was hurt, but the Source Code of my reality was instantly corrupted.

There is no manual for the weight of knowing you've derailed someone else's trajectory—knowing that their System Error was an output of your own mistake.

The impact was the loudest sound; a violent force that came with severe whiplash. The immediate aftermath wasn't a clean break; it was a slow, agonizing System-wide degradation.

The impact may have lasted seconds, but the Residual Code rewrote a new Operating System. The following Processes became my new reality: depression, self-hatred, and post-traumatic stress disorder.

It wasn't just sadness; it was a Low Power Mode I couldn't exit. The brightness of my world was locked at

One Percent, turning the vibrant Arizona horizon into a Forced Reboot.

To the outside world, I seemed normal. I smiled at the right times. I spoke the right lines. But it was a Static Image—a screensaver designed to hide the fact that the OS underneath was burning.

I always had success with efficiency: hitting milestones before the clock ran out, outrunning the specter of failure. But the architecture had a fatal flaw: it was never reinforced for a collision.

When the accident happened, it didn't just shatter the success; it rendered the wreckage into a permanent, unalterable file. Everything was either a Success or Failure.

SYSTEM_STATUS_REPORT: 02:00 am

Uptime: 19 hours (No Sleep Detected).

Primary Thread: *Self_Hatred.exe* (Running at 99% Capacity).

Background Processes: Flashbacks.

Display Settings: *The Pain In Her Eyes.*

Connection Status: Reality_Server NOT FOUND.

Memory: Crash_Data_2023.Log.

Warning: System Overheating. Critical Failure Imminent.

At 2:00 am, the Arizona desert is supposed to be Silent, Still, and Vast, but the noise was deafening. My mind could not Power Down.

The Source Code of my past was replaying against the dark walls of the room. The Uptime was a lie; I hadn't been "up" for nineteen hours—I had been "haunted" for nineteen hours.

Every time I closed my eyes, the Primary Thread took over. *Self_Hatred.exe* wasn't just a Program; it was a Recursive Script.

It spent every waking second searching for User Errors and finding them in the way I breathed, the way I spoke, and the way I had let that Fatal Exception happen in the first place.

This was not my first car accident; it was my second. Not only that, it was the second that was my fault.

After both, all I could see was the replay. Not only when my eyes were closed, but when they were open. It was a movie without a pause option.

Chapter 10 | Terminal Error

No Recovery Found

Forest Home, a Christian Family Camp, is the epitome of where the best memories of my life were written. The place that has been integrated into my life. For nineteen years, this place held nothing but the kind of memories you could only dream of.

It was the vacation to look forward to every summer, and the place that housed the best shakes in the world. There were Weber-Cummins incidents—family traditions and chaotic memories we would tell for the rest of our lives.

Lifeguard training was a Rigorous Stress Test. The summer of 2024 was nothing but high-level trauma from severe accidents that occurred throughout the first weeks of June. To sum it up: a drowning, broken bones, severe physiological exhaustion, and critical dehydration and starvation.

Initializing day one of Family Camp: three female lifeguards and two male lifeguards were on duty. In a moment of playful laughter and high emotions, the atmosphere shifted instantly. Every sound of laughter was replaced with the sound of screaming.

The Security Protocols were no longer a drill.

It took all five lifeguards to calm the gravity of this situation. Prior to when the male guards could breach the water, the victim's survival instinct triggered a Critical Override—he began using the three girls as leverage, pushing them under the surface to keep his own head above water.

It was a System Conflict where one life was unintentionally compromising three others. The girls were being suppressed and submerged in a loop of desperation until the male guards intervened and forced a Manual Override to break his grip. In the end, the recovery protocols were successful, and everyone was okay—which is what matters.

This summer was a series of Unchecked Exceptions. There were countless instances where another girl got extremely hurt—she almost died—I got hurt, and for the first time, the magic from the place my entire childhood was spent felt like a Corrupted File. One that was unrecoverable.

You'd blink, and another injury was logged; you'd stop to catch your breath, and the sirens of an ambulance would puncture the silence.

By the end of that summer, every speck of joy and high-definition memories I thought would last a lifetime felt like they had been Forcefully Deleted.

Until I was nineteen, this camp was the most heartwarming place where memories were created and stored every summer. From family camp to lifeguarding and other various programs, I had spent nearly every summer of my life in the most magical, memory-filled place.

To watch and feel every good thing disappear was heartbreaking. For it all to feel like it had ended in one summer—where everything went so wrong, so fast—there are no words. I had a front-row seat watching a huge part of my life fall apart. For the first time, it was the last place I wanted to be.

I wanted to press Force Quit.

Chapter 11

Force Launch

[Force_Launch.exe]

Two months apart. Two separate instances of severe, catastrophic negligence. Two girls whose lives were violently Stress-Tested by a staff who treated safety like an optional Protocol.

May 28, 2024 | The summer hadn't even started. We were on our last week of lifeguard training. It was "break the rules" day at the lake for staff—a day where standard safety protocols were thrown in the garbage. There is a difference between bending the rules and throwing them away.

My boss and a coworker wanted to double-blob me. The math was a catastrophe—I weighed 120 pounds. Between the two of them—two grown men—they were bringing nearly 300 pounds of combined pressure down on the opposite end.

As we walked up the stairs, we joked about it, but the reality of the physics settled in. I changed my mind. I looked at them and said a direct, unequivocal Nevermind. I knew there was no way.

They agreed to compromise—one of them would jump. I still didn't want it, because the math was a guaranteed horror film, but I was pressured into accepting it. I didn't believe it would just be one of them. That entire time, I should have trusted how I felt because I knew both were going to jump.

I was not wrong.

If I spoke up and defended how I felt, I would have been given every reason why I should follow through, which had already happened, so I did. I don't know how to put into words what three hundred pounds of pressure felt like. It is not something you can explain or find the words to speak. All I know is it was indescribable. A force so great no one should ever know it.

Though I can't explain it, I can still feel the pressure two years later. I think about it, and I feel it. I talk about it, I feel it. I regret it, I feel it. I remember it, I feel it. I think about the Christian Family Camp that was the best part of my life until that summer, and guess what? I feel it. It's awful.

Not just pressure, but height, I still feel the height. I couldn't see it myself, but later, people told me I cleared the tree line. I only had it described to me as that I was significantly higher. People could see it but not feel it. I could feel it but not see it.

I was in the air for so long. After a thought crossed my mind, such as *why am I still in the air?* You guessed it,

I was still airborne. Waiting for my two-hour flight to land was a dreadful sensation, knowing pain was seconds away.

I was so high that I had zero control over how I landed. I landed on my back. I had the realization that I was dead—because water felt like solid concrete, but then I knew if I were, I wouldn't be able to think about it.

As I reached the surface, I thought I broke my back; I almost did. My neck hurt so much. There was severe bruising and pain, which lasted for weeks. This was not a quick feel-normal escalation.

It hurt really badly to walk, and it hurt so much to breathe. Sleep was horrible. I honestly think something happened (obviously not a broken back), but the pain and the longevity explain it was likely more serious than me brushing it off.

July | The environment was concrete. Another girl, but the same overlooked safety protocol. The blob wasn't in the lake; it was dragged onto the grass, fully inflated, and positioned completely unprotected. This time, it wasn't two men.

It was five grown adults sprinting and launching themselves onto the blown-up blob at full force while she sat on the end. There are videos of this, and I really don't know why. I was not at the lake on this day; I was at the pool, so I only know from what I've heard, seen, and general common sense.

An expulsion.

Her height was less, but she wasn't falling toward a deep lake. Her landing zone was pavement. The idea everyone had was that she wouldn't be propelled forward and would just land safely back on the blob. With it fully inflated, good luck. It acted like a springboard with zero cushion.

She was unconscious on impact. She was rushed to the hospital and was there for weeks. Her damage was physical—mine was broken in the silence that followed. So many important things were overlooked this summer—Safety Protocols, Avoidable Events, etc.

It is one thing to survive an accident; it is entirely different to survive a cause of negligence. Looking back at the entirety of that summer, the most haunting realization is that almost none of it had to happen.

These were not unpredictable acts of nature. They were not unavoidable tragedies. They were the direct, mathematical result of humans looking at a Redlining System, acknowledging the "check engine" light, and deciding to press the gas pedal anyway.

Safety protocols exist for a reason. They are the hardcoded firewalls designed to prevent a crash. For the duration of the 2024 season, those protocols were treated like the "Terms and Conditions" on a software update—everyone blindly clicked Accept without reading the Warnings.

The hardest pill to swallow is the word Avoidable. If the blob had stayed in the water while playing, a girl wouldn't have spent weeks in a hospital. If the math of a 120-pound girl versus 300 pounds of force had been respected, I wouldn't have had to beg for air.

Negligence didn't stop with the physical accidents; it bled into the everyday operation of the camp. We were functioning in a completely unsustainable loop. After witnessing trauma, experiencing trauma, and running on corrupted sleep, there was zero recovery protocol.

If a computer crashes, you reboot it. If a human crashes, you give them time to heal. But in this environment, a crash was an inconvenience to the schedule. I almost broke my back, and the immediate response was not a medical check, an incident report, or a day of rest. The response was: Right away, it was back to getting things ready for the start of camp.

We were tasked with keeping everyone else alive while our own internal batteries were blinking at one percent. And instead of letting us power down at the end of the day, we were authorized to clock back in from 2:00 to 4:00 am to run laser tag and staff paintball wars through the dark, freezing mountains for hours on end.

Even with all the disasters, nothing paused. We were expected to push through the dark, running on minutes of sleep, surrounded by unexplainable things that had happened to us that are not talked about today.

Chapter 12 | System Lag

University v1.1

Sophomore year was supposed to be the System Reset. After the Catastrophic System Crash of the summer, I was looking for a clean Install—a Fresh Start where the code wasn't corrupted by sirens and a "Force Quit."

I moved into a high-spec, modern apartment with two other girls, a configuration that was perfect on paper.

I was convinced that v1.1 was going to be the update where life ran smoothly. What I didn't realize was that I was experiencing a False Positive.

At 4:00 am, the night before classes began, an unauthorized background process took over what should have been sleep. A party loud enough to redline the apartment's hardware.

There was alcohol and underage drinking. Non-compliant protocols I wanted zero part of. I felt so awful that I was in the same place, though I had no idea. What made it worse was this was at a Christian university I was so ready for.

From the girls I lived with, I was stuck in a year-long situation, cleaning up every mess and fault. This was a persistent, continuous Environmental Error that initiated total mental and physical exhaustion. I would so often find myself in a Low-Level Maintenance cycle on my hands and knees scrubbing the hardware of our apartment, because if I didn't, no one would. It was a constant background process that triggered multiple times every single day.

No responsibility or ownership was logged on their end. I was perpetually stuck in the middle, trying to make sure everything stayed okay.

Although they were very nice girls, or that was a placeholder slide designed to hide a messy backend, they showed zero respect for others because of the choices they made that affected those around them, not just me.

Every conversation they had was a high-decibel System Alert that no one could turn down, eventually becoming cached audio that stayed stuck in my head for months. I only experienced silence when their status was set to offline.

On March 1st, 2025, my family and I suffered the loss of our childhood dog. She had been integrated into my life since I was five years old—fifteen years of uninterrupted uptime. I had no idea what life was like without her until that day.

In the months that followed, life felt so empty, and it seemed so impossible to do anything. I would show up to classes unable to hold back tears.

For months, I felt so numb to everything. My battery was at 1%, from so much exhaustion that didn't take one second off. The only thing I wanted at this point was to lie on the floor of a dark room and never get up.

Everything felt really hard because a huge part of my life no longer existed.

Sophomore year was the definition of Low-Power Status, a depression that only intensified as my world collapsed. Days felt like weeks; weeks felt like months. The reality of loss is a Sharp Signal that never dissipates. In my life thus far, I have logged four—the first at age 12, followed by 17, 18, and 19.

Chapter 13

255 Feet of Dead Air

[Timestamp: February 15, 2025 | Six Flags]

It started with my seat restraint breaking at the summit of a 255-foot vertical drop.

If you've ever been on a mega-coaster, you know the sound of the ascent. It's that slow, agonizing, mechanical noise that gives you way too much time to think about your life choices.

A lap bar is a generalized restraint; it doesn't contour to you. As the coaster tipped over the edge, I felt it. A distinct, terrifying volume of space between my body and the heavy plastic that was supposed to keep me anchored to the earth. It left nothing but dead air between me and terminal velocity.

Any normal person in this situation might scream in pure terror or clutch the bar for dear life. I, however, was genuinely unsure if my life was going to end in the next three seconds, but because roller coaster incidents are a main experience, I did the only logical thing.

As gravity took over and I actively levitated out of my seat, hovering in that dead air, I threw my hands up and yelled, "*Weee!*"

If I was going out, I was going out on brand.

The lap bar caught me enough to keep me from launching into the next zip code, and we finally hit the brake run.

It isn't supposed to happen twice—the same hour, two situations that had fatal potential. The second occurrence, the roller coaster directly after—at the exact moment gravity was trying to rip us toward the pavement, the hydraulic "shoulder" restraint over my cousin failed.

Her only option was to force it down through the gravitational pulls and high-speed momentum. I felt so unexplainably awful. It's one thing when a roller coaster incident happens to me, whatever. When it happens to someone else, I have no words.

I survived the dead air on the 255-foot vertical drop. She survived the disengaged hydraulic lock.

We walked away from shattered safety.

Chapter 14

Data Migration

Initiating a two-month Study Abroad Deployment to the other side of the world was so much fun. Seven weeks, seven countries. It was a high-definition Stress Test, which you guys should know, I love. Two classes, each sixteen weeks of work compressed into three weeks.

I studied at a Christian university on the other side of the world in Klaipeda, Lithuania. While the city was gorgeous and looked like heaven, the environmental conditions were treacherous—a harsh simulation where temperatures were freezing, and winds remained at a constant, high redline.

I have the best memories from this university, which I am so grateful to be able to say, considering the experiences that took place prior to studying abroad.

The night we left for London, England, we encountered a major Routing Error: our Uber dropped us off outside the woods. This was not where the drop-off location was set. Do not ask me how this happened.

No other Transport Protocols were available in that area, and we were dropped off the grid. We were forced into a Manual Hardware Transport, lugging suitcases across the woods inches away from the road, trying to avoid a System Collision with cars on the narrow shoulder.

We couldn't stop laughing; three girls lugging suitcases as if we were walking across the entire country. It was so hilarious because of how dangerous it was. We landed in London at 2:00 am, which felt surreal.

We booked all the tours and hit a Broadway show. Even during days of heavy pouring rain, we stayed online, doing everything while completely soaked—the best moments of my life.

The drop-off error wasn't the last incident. It was the first. While we were in Estonia, we decided to hike up a mountain, though it was pouring and nearly thundering.

I do not know what architectural logic dictates paving a vertical incline with smooth, rounded stones, but it is a Structural Hazard that defies all safety protocols. It was incredibly steep—a punishing, relentless upward grade that felt less like a hike and more like a punishment.

The descent is where gravity stops being a resistance and becomes a threat. On the way down, the pouring rain transformed the steep, cobblestone path from a difficult hike into a frictionless nightmare. It was like trying to navigate a steep staircase of wet ice. Every step was a calculated risk, an attempt to find traction where none existed.

The path we were required to take bordered the edge of the mountain. There were no guardrails, no

Chapter 15

Security Breach

I had been at our home in Malibu for two weeks. On July 29th, 2025, there was a violent break-in robbery. That morning, there was a huge spider under the sheets of my bed. I had zero logical reason to leave that day, and I honestly didn't want to, but that single interrupt prompted me to relocate my life for the evening.

That is the reason I was not home. I left twenty minutes before the incident. I would not have left had I not flagged a spider earlier that morning. As traumatizing as that event was, it played a role that potentially saved my life.

I had no idea that a terrifying environmental situation was actually sparing me. God definitely knew what He was doing with that one. Because everyone thought I was home, just imagine the notifications from people unsure if I was okay.

The worst place you could be while this scenario occurs is a place where your phone is turned off for a long period of time. I had no idea what was happening for three hours. So, to learn from that, I should never book a movie after a spider tries to murder me.

These events occurred while my family was scattered over the world. I was the only person at our Malibu house for two weeks. It was an open crime scene where shoes were left on the roof along with energy drink cans and forced entry.

Bags were aggressively tossed, personal items were rummaged through, and this turned into an open investigation. To get a call where your entire life felt violated was a feeling words can't describe. That was one of the worst nights of my life.

Chapter 16

Optical Recognition

There is a difference between being looked at and being seen. For years, I perfected the art of passing every test of Optical Recognition—smiling at the right times, laughing all the time, looking people in the eye—all while the truth remained hidden in front of them.

It was an exhausting choreography. Every social interaction felt like a performance where the stakes were my survival. I became a master of the "surface-level"—ensuring that if anyone glanced my way, they saw exactly what they expected to see: a girl who was happy, engaged, and entirely "fine." The performance was flawless, but the act was killing me.

Smiling wasn't the issue; it was the haunting effort of acting as though the happiness behind it was real. I was a master at the display, but I was dying under the deception. The worst part was that the performance didn't end when the door shut. It had become so deeply engraved that an "off" switch never existed.

If the girl the world saw was "fine," then the girl sitting in the dark had to be "fine" too. The saddest part about a flawless performance is that no one looks for the person behind it. Although the pain never shut off, there was a filter I always chose to use. Over time, that filter became my only reality. I had successfully navigated the act; perfectly composed, entirely “fine,” and completely numb. It felt like a protective fog that kept the warmth of the world in front of me—visible, but untouchable.

I wasn't just tired; I was depleted. I had given so much energy to the display that I had nothing left for the girl it was supposed to protect. The colors of life hadn't just faded; they had been bleached by the constant glare of the stage lights I refused to turn off.

I had been so successful that I had effectively spent my soul to pay for my reputation.

I almost bought the world’s approval at the expense of my life.

There came a time when I was running out of the power required to act. I had people ask if I was okay all the time. To protect them, I answered yes.

I lied to keep the world of others warm while mine was freezing. They were talking to the girl who was “fine,” while the real girl was shivering in a winter they couldn't imagine.

Chapter 17 | System Reboot

University v2

Junior year of college, I initiated a transfer to a new university in Southern California. At first, it is difficult to determine if a new environment feels good because it is new or because it is the right configuration. It turned out to be an Incorrect Status.

I stayed at this university for six weeks before I flagged the Error. Because I was experiencing depression at an unexplainable level, I acted as though everything actually felt okay. An act that was a lie.

The pain I did not want people to know existed. Meanwhile, I felt frozen, unable to catch my breath from crying, and hope felt nonexistent. I had no expectations for this version of my life; I had turned off the Expectation Protocol. The start of October was when I experienced a Termination Signal—suicidal ideation.

To override that urge, I resorted to self-harm—to shift the mental agony into a localized physical pain. Pain I felt like I deserved. I only did this on my stomach. It was the only place where no one would know. When I'd post, no one could know, and in real life, no one knew.

I had waited so long to report the crash that I felt that I had reached a point where I could not see myself alive in twenty minutes. I know I made myself feel so much worse by handling everything alone.

I have a life with the most amazing people in it, which is also a reason I felt I needed to spare them. I didn't want to dim their brightness. If you compare wanting to end everything or continue life, I genuinely wanted to live, but the alternative was the only option where life felt like it would be okay.

Mental health is so serious. It should never be overlooked. For me, it wasn't. It was completely because I stayed quiet, never said anything, and tried saving anyone from the reality I felt. I say mental health should never be overlooked for those who ask for help, and the Support Protocol fails them, potentially causing the end of their life.

There are times when people feel like a permanent solution is the only option. I want people to rely on the fact that when hope feels lost, it doesn't mean it is. To turn from only believing how you feel and looking at the objective of life is a game-changer. A lot of the time, how you feel isn't a full representation of the Source Code—even in the darkest hour, the truth remains: Data Available.

Chapter 18

Recursive Error

During that time, I was so exhausted. I knew it stemmed from something deep—a broken sensation fueled by past events—but I wasn't yet ready to put a name on it. For too long, I had felt as though I was the reason people got hurt—as if the world would fall apart if I didn't put myself through hell. In high school, I would study for hours before allowing myself to eat a meal or drink a glass of water.

It felt as though I didn't deserve the simplest comforts unless I completed a massive, invisible checklist. For years, I believed that if I didn't keep my life perfectly together, people would get hurt. None of this is logical, but the feelings are so visceral. The pervasive feeling was that people were being harmed because of me. Even though that never actually happened, it always felt entirely plausible.

It was incredibly difficult to shake the belief that I could have prevented tragedy. I recall one night, driving home, when I saw a girl banging violently on the passenger-side window of another car. Her face was hidden, but it seemed obvious she was experiencing domestic violence. There is a chance it was something else, but it didn't look that way. I called 911 because it felt like the odds of her being okay were non-existent, given what I had just witnessed. I could not stop crying—partly out of concern for her, and partly as a form of self-punishment for not being able to stop it.

Five weeks later, I pulled into a parking lot minutes after someone had just been run over. They were lying on the ground, clearly not okay. It was jarring to face that reality, especially having witnessed two situations of severe harm so close together.

Every bad thing feels like it's on you. It's not about playing the victim; it's about the crushing weight of believing you could have changed the outcome.

For three years, I felt like I was the reason people got cancer.

From 2022 through October 2025, no one in the world knew. I never said anything. We had three family members get diagnosed and pass away. Seventeen was the first time I felt that way, until twenty. It felt like Satan was tormenting me.

It was a state of constant, unrelenting exhaustion—physical, mental, and behavioral. There were times I would be lying on the floor of the shower, unable to fathom opening my eyes.

I never felt there was time to relax; I was always ensuring everyone else was safe. At the time, I didn't realize how exhausted I was because my drive to protect others kept me going. I felt I couldn't stop to focus on myself because if I did, the world would come crashing down.

I felt the weight of the world on my shoulders for years. By October 2, 2025, I felt that if I weren't alive, everyone and everything would finally be okay.

I figured the risk of people getting hurt would vanish if I wasn't there to trigger it. At the time, it felt like there was nothing left to live for. This echoed the unexplainable depression I described in Chapter Seventeen.

Although I feel so grateful for the life I have, for a long time, everything felt so faded out. I was also extremely uncomfortable at my university, which magnified the problem. It was the third university I had attended in the first two years of college.

It felt like ending my life was the only viable option. I did not want to die, but it felt like other people's lives remained at risk if I existed. It's insane how easy it is to walk through hell with a smile.

And there it was. The word for the chaos I couldn't name: Obsessive Compulsive Disorder.

Chapter 19

Runtime Error

Something you never think would happen to you. October 27, 2025. My family and I were celebrating my dad's birthday. That night, we were walking the streets of Hollywood when terror played out right in front of us.

My mom and I were on the side closest to the street, walking with our arms around each other. I do not recall where the rest of the family was, or who was behind or in front of us. There was lots of conversation, laughter, and a genuinely happy family. It was a second that changed everything—or easily could have.

The peace, the laughter, and the happiness we all felt were instantly shattered.

In a horrific moment, a man very aggressively threw his entire weight into us, striking my mom's shoulder with two hard hits.

Because we had our arms around each other, the impact hit us both. The violent force pushed her into me, and we both fell into Hollywood Boulevard. My mom fell first, hitting the pavement harder.

Time dragged as she hit the ground.

As I fell, I thought I saw her hit her head on the asphalt. For one agonizing, breathless second as she landed—I was certain I was watching her die.

When time snapped back into motion, silence was replaced by screaming. I don't even know who it came from first—if it was my family, the street, or my own voice.

The trauma of that night didn't end with the physical impact. What immediately followed was an aggressive verbal attack that felt just as violent. The man who hit us didn't run in a panic, and he didn't freeze in shock.

He walked away.

Looking back at the situation he caused every now and then while cursing us out with everything he had—physical, verbal, and emotional assault.

Chapter 20

The Thawing

Aftershock—for half a year, this was the only sensation I felt. It isn't peaceful, and it isn't restful. It is the process of a circuit breaker turning back on after being forcefully shut off.

When that night of my life happened, I unintentionally made myself feel—nothing. I could hear when he screamed at us from the shadows. I could see how dangerous the situation was. But I was pretending like I was not the girl who lived it.

So, I shut the power off.

From October 27th until the warmth of April finally broke through the winter, I never felt like I had been physically assaulted. If you had asked me during those six months what happened, I could tell you the date. I could tell you the location. I could tell you detail by detail.

But did I feel like the girl who lived it? No.

I convinced myself that because I wasn't falling apart, I was "fine." I thought my lack of tears after so long was proof of my resilience. Now, half a year later, the protective fog is lifting. It took so long because I never spoke about it, wrote about it, or read about it. Until now, I kept the silence intact.

Putting that night into words broke the seal.

Because I kept it so quiet, I have no idea who is reading this already knowing what happened, and who is finding out for the first time.

When it felt as though there was fog around this night, I felt safe. I knew those events existed, but I couldn't see them clearly. There was a warm distance between me and every second of the tragedy that was, and the tragedy that could have been.

I was twenty years old. And in a single, violent second, I was physically, verbally, and emotionally assaulted by a stranger who looked at us and decided we were collateral damage for whatever rage he was holding in.

Remembering the evil in his voice as he cursed us out, realizing that he meant to break us.

Knowing that at twenty, I can no longer say I have never been physically assaulted.

I never imagined that would be a question I couldn't answer "no" to. I felt myself mourning the girl I was on October 26, the girl who could say "no" to that question—the girl who walked down Hollywood Boulevard and never made it to the other side.

I think about how safe we thought we were when we had no idea we weren't. To have that pure, safe moment shattered so violently breaks my heart every time. The street was just a lively backdrop to my dad's birthday. That night became a hijacked celebration, timestamped for tragedy.

We weren't just robbed of a perfect evening; we were robbed of the baseline assumption that we could walk alongside each other without bracing for impact.

When she fell, my sense of security fell with her. The girl who was walking before the assault—the one who didn't scan the pavement, who didn't flinch at sudden movements, who couldn't fathom a human treating anyone like collateral damage—never made it to the end of the block.

There is a silent, global community of people—mostly women, though not exclusively—who know exactly what this feels like. Those who survived assault, and much worse, who turned off all their circuit breakers to feel safe enough, only to have everything turn on during a random Thursday months or years later.

If you are reading this and recognize that specific loss of light, I want you to know I see you. There is a profound, isolating exhaustion that comes with walking through the world pretending your baseline of safety hasn't been permanently altered.

You might be carrying the physical and emotional weight of your own hijacked moments, smiling through daily routines while silently bracing for an impact that has already happened. If you are mourning the version of yourself who used to walk without scanning the pavement, who used to exist without the cold, sudden awareness of human fragility, you are not broken for missing the lightness you lost.

You are absolutely not alone in the heavy, sinking weight you carry now. And when the circuit breaker finally turns back on, I want you to know that the sudden rush of pain doesn't mean you are regressing. It doesn't mean you are weak.

It means you are safe enough to feel it.

Chapter 21

Hardcoded Expectations

Our generation is haunted by toxic beauty standards that make it feel nearly impossible to exist as you are. It is mentally and physically exhausting to strive for the unattainable. We live in a world where "fake" is preferred because fake is perfect.

Social media is such a toxic place to be tied to constantly. Most things that are posted are an expectation of life where hardships aren't talked about, or are often filtered. Social media is a highlight reel, not a reality check. Especially as a girl in this generation, there is a perceived obligation to meet insane standards, despite the lack of realistic foundations behind them.

Comparison is the plague of our era. It is so easy to get lost in the "what ifs" instead of finding contentment in what is. It is unfair to feel forced to live up to the world's expectations rather than living for yourself. It is an exhausting feat to obsess over details that could be "perfect," only to realize you are pouring immense effort into things that others may never notice.

There is always more work to do, another standard to meet, another bar to clear. This is no way to live. Social media has no concept of the work you put into meeting these standards in real life, so it deserves none of your energy. I will admit that there are standards I have kept up with—but I have learned to distinguish between what I do for the world and what I do for myself. Archive the expectations you don't enjoy. It is your life, not theirs. You should be the primary beneficiary of your own existence. This is difficult, especially if you struggle with a deep-seated need to present perfectly to others.

But we have to ask: can our generation drop these over-the-top, useless expectations that we hold ourselves accountable to? We owe it to ourselves, but we also owe it to the generations following us. They are already picking up the pressures rooted in today's society. If we don't press pause now, they will be the ones forced to live up to them tomorrow.

Chapter 22

Multi-Threaded

From the day I was born, spiders have been my worst fear and, of course, my most frequent stalkers. I have seen such an inconceivable amount in the twenty years I have been alive that it has begun to feel targeted. Let me rephrase that, it is targeted.

There have been an unspeakable number of times when I'm driving, and a spider attacks me. I am genuinely shocked I've never been in a car accident for this reason, as a sudden arachnid occupant is exactly what would cause one. I've found them under garage-door keypads countless times and in places so unthinkable they defy logic.

I'm not exaggerating when I say every time I came home from college, there was a spider encounter within minutes of my arrival; sometimes it was seconds.

In July, there was a huge spider on the ground. I couldn't bring myself to kill it properly, so I vacuumed it. I have no idea how this happened, but minutes later, I felt like I was dying. This encounter was so traumatic that I was physically sick to my stomach. I literally lost my voice for the next two weeks.

When I was younger, my family bought a huge animatronic tarantula and tortured me, which should not sound shocking. Mind you, I was a ten-year-old girl. Ten. So often this tarantula was the first thing I saw when I woke up—they'd put it on my bed, leave it outside my door, or have Jake chase me through Hathaway.

In all fairness, though, my hamster killed his hamster, so I owed him. Honestly.

To make matters worse, that was not the first pet I owned that had an urge to kill. Our golden retriever, Cooper, killed a bunny on Easter this year. In what lifetime does a girl own two pets that are murderers? Like, I did NOT raise them to do that, I swear.

Other family members probably did.

It was one hundred percent unintentional, but it was one of those things that ends in worst case scenario. If you know Goldens, they are the absolute best thing on earth. Never would they intentionally cause harm to another animal. Hamsters, I cannot say the same. My hamster had heinous intentions, which played out successfully, unfortunately.

Rest in peace, Jake's hamster. I'm so sorry.

Back to my stalkers, the frequency is insane. Once, I found two huge spiders in the same spot, inches apart. I went downstairs to the kitchen and found a third. I went back upstairs immediately, and around the corner—just feet from the first two—was a fourth.

That is four spiders in sixty seconds. This was not the first time there was a batch of three or more; it was the second. Earlier that week, there were three huge spiders within inches of each other, not to mention two were on top of each other. Excuse me? Like, sorry for invading a moment. Were they trying to copy and paste themselves? I have photographic evidence of this event. I can't wait to present it to my legal team.

There is no way this isn't a statistical anomaly. No one can do anything about it, though; you can't guarantee you'll never see them. It has become a matter of acceptance.

It happens so often that walking into a room where a spider descends from the ceiling is so normal. I'm shocked when that doesn't happen. I have eyewitnesses and time-stamped photo proof for many of these situations because it sounds so frequent that people can easily assume I'm lying.

I've had dreams where spiders are the only thing present, only to wake up and see them in real life. If I see a spider on Instagram, I can almost guarantee I'll see one in real-time. If I dare to speak the word "Spider," the same thing happens.

Spiders are giving me a reason to talk. If they want me to stop, they should stop giving me material. I kept my mouth shut for nineteen years about how often this was happening, avoiding social media rants.

But in real life, everyone knows this happens to me as often as you breathe. I have no idea what it's like to go two days without seeing them.

A spider-free life is a luxury I have rarely experienced.

It feels so unfair to know that I have to mention spiders on my wedding day. I literally have to incorporate this in my vows because I know this won't ever stop.

It's reached such a high point where I have to "legalize" the situation in my marriage contract; my husband has to sign off on the Terms and Conditions that come with me.

There's no day off—not even my own wedding—so I might as well make the situation clear from the start. I'm already so deeply sorry for my future husband and the volume of spiders he is destined to kill.

This has only worsened as I've gotten older. I freak out less—it's easy to have no reaction when you're so used to it—but the frequency has grown tremendously.

I'm so sick of this magnitude of attraction.

Everyone who knows me knows this is a huge part of my life. My family could talk for hours about the encounters they've witnessed without me saying a word.

Can I sue spiders for emotional damage? I'd seriously make them a deal—I'll give them anything they want if they let me live a life where they aren't a lead character.

I need them to stop being so attracted to me so I can enjoy my life.

And I need them to leave my future husband and family alone, too. If this follows me into my future home, I'm filing a class-action lawsuit against the entire Araneae order. I'll see you in court.

END-USER LICENSE AGREEMENT (EULA): THE CUMMINS-SPIDER PROTOCOL

Version: 2026.1.1

Subject: Marriage Contract Appendix A

Parties: The Author ("User") and The Future Husband ("System Administrator")

SCOPE OF ATTRACTION The System Administrator acknowledges that the User is a statistical anomaly regarding the order *Araneae.* Encounters are to be expected in unthinkable locations, including but not limited to:

- **Moving Vehicles:** Spiders are authorized to initiate surprise attacks while the User is operating a motor vehicle. The System Administrator is responsible for post-incident vehicle stabilization.
- **Sanctuary Zones:** Expect localized incursions under bed sheets, behind garage-door keypads, and in any location that defies logical explanation.
- **Vertical Incursions:** Spiders descending from the ceiling upon the User's entry into a room, a phenomenon categorized as "normal" operational behavior within the User's environment.
- **The "Copy-Paste" Glitch:** The System Administrator must be prepared for spiders to "Copy and Paste" themselves, appearing in batches of three, sometimes stacked on top of each other.
- **Recursive Batches:** Groups of four or more appearing within sixty-second intervals.

AUTOMATIC TRIGGER EVENTS The System Administrator should be aware that certain User actions act as an "Instant Spawn" command for real-world entries:

- **Social Media Latency:** Viewing a spider on Instagram acts as a 1:1 digital-to-physical Rendering Command. If it is on the screen, it is in the room.
- **Vocal Activation:** Speaking the word "Spider" triggers an immediate System Update where an arachnid appears in real life.

BIO-HAZARD DISCLOSURE: THE "MURDERER PET" CLAUSE The System Administrator acknowledges that the User's environment has a history of hosting pets with "heinous intentions." This includes:

- **Hamster Conflict:** Previous hardware (User's hamster) successfully terminated a sibling unit's hamster.
- **Golden Retriever Anomalies:** Despite being the "best thing on earth," units like Cooper have been known to engage in holiday-themed terminations (Easter bunnies).

ADMINISTRATOR RESPONSIBILITIES & EMERGENCY PROCEDURES (THE "KILL ORDER") By signing the marriage contract, the System Administrator agrees to the following mandatory protocols:

- **Active Defense:** The Administrator is responsible for the permanent deletion (removal) of all spiders within the User's vicinity.
- **Zero Downtime:** This obligation remains active 24/7/365. There are no "days off," including the wedding day and subsequent anniversaries.

- **Advanced Disposal:** Vacuuming is strictly Prohibited due to high risk of traumatic Hardware Failure. Past attempts have resulted in a Hardware Crash, including the User physically losing her voice for two weeks.
- **Family Stress-Test Disclaimer:** The User has been subjected to historical trauma involving animatronic tarantulas placed in beds by sibling "units." As a result, any "prank" involving arachnids will be considered a breach of this contract and may result in immediate litigation.

DISCLOSURES

- **High-Frequency Signal:** A spider-free life is a luxury the User has rarely experienced. The Administrator should expect a Minimum window of two days between sightings.
- **Social Media Trigger:** Mentioning or viewing spiders on digital platforms acts as a "Spawn Command" for real-time encounters.
- **Evidence Logs:** All encounters are backed by time-stamped photographic proof and eyewitness logs for use in future litigation.

LIMITATION OF LIABILITY The User shall not be held liable for emotional damage or high-volume Alerts triggered by eight-legged hardware breaches.

- **Hearing Protection:** The System Administrator reserves the right to sue for hearing damage caused by the volume of the User's "Security Alerts" (screaming).
- **Emotional Distress:** The User reserves the right to seek damages for emotional distress against the entire *Araneae* order in a future class-action lawsuit.

THE "TIL DEATH DO US PART (OR UNTIL SPIDERS TAKE US OUT)" CLAUSE Failure to mitigate the frequency of these encounters may result in a class-action lawsuit filed by the User against the entire *Araneae* order. I'll see you in court.

BY PROCEEDING TO THE ALTAR, THE SYSTEM ADMINISTRATOR ACCEPTS THESE TERMS AND CONDITIONS.

User Note: I am so deeply sorry for the volume of spiders you are destined to kill. I've got a lawsuit.

APPENDIX B: THE WEBER-CUMMINS LEGAL ARCHIVE

File Status: OPEN / RECURSIVE

Lead Counsel: Caitlin Cummins

EXHIBIT 1: CLASS-ACTION COMPLAINT

Court: Superior Court of Araneae Order

Plaintiff: Caitlin Cummins

Defendant: The Taxonomic Order *Araneae* (Spiders)

1. UNAUTHORIZED BATCH PROCESSING The Plaintiff submits evidence of "Recursive Spawning," wherein Defendants appear in batches of four within sixty-second intervals. Specifically, Plaintiff logs a "Copy-Paste Glitch" where two units were found stacked directly on top of each other in a vertical configuration.

2. VEHICULAR AMBUSH & HARDWARE INTERFERENCE Defendants are accused of initiating "High-Speed Attacks" during motor vehicle operation. This behavior is categorized as a "Hardware Error" that risks catastrophic car accidents.

3. LOSS OF AUDIO OUTPUT (THE VACUUM INCIDENT) In July 2025, a hardware conflict involving a vacuum resulted in the Plaintiff suffering a loss of vocal output for a duration of fourteen (14) days.

EXHIBIT 2: DEPOSITION OF THE "MURDERER" UNITS

Subject: Character Witnesses and Biological Liabilities

Witness 1: "Cooper" (Golden Retriever Unit) Testimony: Despite being categorized as "the absolute best thing on earth," Witness has a documented history of "holiday-themed terminations," specifically regarding a bunny on Easter.

- **Liability:** Witness is incapable of "intentional harm" but remains a risk to low-profile biological units.

Witness 2: "The Hamster" (Deceased/Legacy Hardware) Testimony: Plaintiff admits that her legacy hardware (the hamster) possessed "heinous intentions."

- **Evidence:** Said unit Successfully performed a "permanent deletion" on a sibling unit's (Jake's) hamster hardware.

EXHIBIT 3: TSA SECURITY ADVISORY (INTERNATIONAL)

Ref: Parent-Unit Incarceration Risk

1. NON-COMPLIANT PACKING PROTOCOLS Be advised that Maternal units have a high-frequency risk of "Unintentional Packing Errors."

2. SEIZED HARDWARE The following items have been flagged as TSA Threats:

- Pocket knives shaped like grenades.
- Pocket knives shaped like firearms.

3. LEGAL MIRACLE STATUS It is hereby logged as a “Statistical Miracle” that the Weber-Cummins alliance has not been banned from all public places or permanently relocated to jail.

EXHIBIT 4: FINAL RESTRAINING ORDER & EULA

Applicable to: The Future Husband (*System Security Specialist*)

1. THE "KILL ORDER" MANDATE By accepting the Marriage Contract, the Specialist agrees to a “zero-downtime” response for spider deletions.

2. CEILING BUFFER ZONE A mandatory 50-Foot buffer is hereby Ordered for all spiders descending from ceilings.

3. WEDDING DAY BLACKOUT A total “System Lockdown” is in effect for the wedding day. No spiders are Permitted within the Sanctuary, regardless of “Attraction” Status.

Chapter 23

Restoration Point

This is the Restoration Point. I've been a Christian my entire life—not because I was born into a Christian family, but because it is the path I chose for myself. It is, without question, the best decision I have ever made.

I was dedicated as a baby, baptized at Forest Home, and again in Israel. I have always strived to strengthen my relationship with Jesus—not just for myself, but for my future husband and family. There have been seasons when the weight of the world felt too heavy to keep in second place, but I have been fortunate to keep God first.

In today's society, so much revolves around worldly desires and material gain. While these are fleeting elements, they are not Life. Our life should never be centered on the attention of the world, but on doing everything through God and for His glory.

Part of why high school was so hard to enjoy was the lack of a Christian dimension. I spent my first year and a half at a public high school, but when I transferred to a private, Christian online school, I loved it because it felt right; I realized then that everything had occurred specifically to lead me there.

Everything that happened in college happened for a reason, whether that reason ever becomes clear or not. It is enough for me to know that God knows why, and I am content to leave it at that.

I have witnessed people accept Jesus Christ and turn from their pasts to follow Him. The world has always needed Jesus, but now more than ever. The most important decision anyone can make is accepting Him—not just turning toward Him, but knowing Him.

Jesus has saved me from countless situations that would have been damaging had they unfolded. I have seen the gift in unanswered prayers—for a university or a relationship—realizing later there was a larger reason those were not in the script.

It is rarely God saying "no"; it is Him protecting you from a "yes" that would have cost you too much. The alternative is that we would be praying for a way out. In my life, the strength required to survive the hardest seasons has come solely from Jesus. It is the only reason I am standing at all.

As I navigate the complexities of this world, I am intentional about prioritizing my relationship with Jesus above all else. In a culture that equates worth with material gain and temporary success, the pressure to conform has been nonexistent by the glory of God.

I have learned that true fulfillment and a lasting sense of purpose are found only in a life lived to honor Him. In a world that feels like it is out of control, I know the message of Jesus Christ is more relevant than ever. Looking back on my life, I see the fingerprints of God's protection and the hand that guided me toward His purpose. I see it in the "no" of unanswered prayers that ultimately led to far better outcomes. I feel it in the strength He granted me when the path ahead was lost in the shadows.

The pain is no longer the story

The Restoration is

Recognitions

To my Family: Thank you for being the steady ground when I was navigating the dark. For trusting how I felt when honesty didn't feel like a choice. Thank you for standing in the wreckage without asking me to hurry through it.

To the Webers: Thank you for providing all the love and support in the world. Having your encouragement throughout the journey of this book—and this life—has meant everything to me. I love you all more than I can put into words.

Mental Health Resources

If the stories in this book resonated with you, or if you find yourself navigating a difficult stretch of your own road, please know that you do not have to drive it alone. Your health is a priority, and there are people ready to help you steer through the storm.

Immediate Crisis Support

If you or someone you know is in immediate danger or experiencing a mental health crisis, please reach out to these 24/7 Services:

988 Suicide & Crisis Lifeline (USA & Canada): Call or text **988**. This is a free, confidential service available anytime.

Crisis Text Line: Text **HOME** to **741741** to connect with a volunteer crisis counselor.

The Trevor Project: Call **1-866-488-7386** or text **START** to **678-678**.

Veterans Crisis Line: Dial **988** and press **1**, or text **838255**.

Finding Professional Help

Connecting with a therapist or counselor can provide the "Roadside Assistance" needed for long-term healing.

Psychology Today Directory: A comprehensive tool to find therapists, psychiatrists, and support groups in your area.

Substance Abuse and Mental Health Services Administration (SAMHSA): For help finding treatment facilities for mental health or substance use disorders.

Support & Education Organizations

These organizations offer a wealth of information to ensure Mental Health is Never Overlooked:

National Alliance on Mental Health (NAMI): Provides advocacy, education, and support group information.

Mental Health America (MHA): Offers screening tools and resources for prevention and early intervention.

Anxiety and Depression Association of America (ADAA): Focuses on the prevention, treatment, and cure of anxiety, depression, and related disorders.

Digital Tools & Apps

For daily maintenance and finding moments of peace in the chaos:

Headspace: Useful for mindfulness and meditation to help you find your "center" during an insane day.

MindShift CBT: Specifically designed to help users manage anxiety using cognitive behavioral therapy techniques.

The Author

Caitlin Cummins is an author and advocate dedicated to making mental health seen. Writing at the intersection of chaos and calm, her work centers on the conviction that mental health is a journey that demands to be shared, not hidden. Though her personal history behind the wheel has been famously insane, the road is precisely where she found the tranquility to speak her truth—using that peace as fuel for a life of advocacy. A resident of Los Angeles, California, she serves as a voice for anyone who has ever felt locked behind a shut door. The Pain in Her Eyes is her debut memoir.

SUPERIOR COURT OF SOUTHERN CALIFORNIA

CAITLIN CUMMINS, *Plaintiff,*

v.

THE TAXONOMIC ORDER ARANEAE, *Defendants.*

Case No: 2026-RECURSIVE-ERROR-01

COMPLAINT FOR EMOTIONAL DAMAGES, SYSTEM BREACH, AND UNAUTHORIZED VERTICAL INCURSION

I. STATEMENT OF FACTS

1. Plaintiff alleges a "hardcoded attraction" that defies all known statistical logic, resulting in a near-daily "high-frequency signal" of spider encounters.
2. **The Instagram Trigger:** Defendants utilize the Plaintiff's digital feed as a "Rendering Command." If a spider is viewed on social media, a physical unit is automatically generated in the Plaintiff's immediate reality.
3. **The Vacuum Incident:** In July 2025, a hardware conflict occurred when Plaintiff attempted to delete a unit via vacuum. This resulted in a total System Crash where Plaintiff lost her vocal output for fourteen days.

II. EXHIBIT A: THE "COPY-PASTE" BUG 4. Plaintiff submits Exhibit A as Primary Evidence of "Recursive Spawning." 5. In February 2026, Plaintiff logged four (4) large spiders within sixty seconds, including a separate instance where two units were "Copy-Pasted" directly on top of each other.

EXHIBIT A: DATA LOG 2025-10 *Description:* Photographic evidence of unauthorized batch processing. Defendants are pictured stacked in a vertical configuration, violating all standard laws of personal space and biological decency.

III. COUNT I: UNAUTHORIZED VERTICAL INCURSION 6. Plaintiff alleges that Defendants consistently utilize "Gravity Overrides" to descend from ceilings upon Plaintiff's entry into a room.

IV. COUNT II: ILLEGAL HARDWARE INTERFERENCE (VEHICULAR) 7. Defendants have repeatedly initiated surprise attacks within motor vehicles while the Plaintiff is in a high-speed operating state, risking catastrophic car accidents.

V. COUNT III: BREACH OF SANCTUARY PROTOCOL 8. Defendants are accused of violating "Safe Mode" by appearing under bed sheets and behind Security Hardware, such as garage-door keypads.

VI. CHARACTER WITNESS DISCLOSURE 9. Plaintiff reserves the right to call upon her support units (the Cummins and Weber families) as eyewitnesses to these unhinged spawning rates. 10. Plaintiff further discloses that her domestic hardware (hamsters and golden retriever) has a documented history of "heinous intentions" and may be hostile toward Defendants.

V. PRAYER FOR RELIEF Plaintiff respectfully requests:

- **Marriage Contract Indemnity:** Full legal recognition that the Plaintiff's future husband is contractually obligated to perform all "Kill Commands" without complaint.
- **Damages:** Compensation for twenty years of emotional damage.

DATED: April 16, 2026

SIGNED: *Caitlin Cummins*

TEMPORARY RESTRAINING ORDER: SYSTEM SECURITY PROTOCOL

TO ALL MEMBERS OF THE ORDER ARANEAE:

Effective immediately, you are hereby **RESTRAINED** and **ENJOINED** from the following activities regarding the individual known as Caitlin Cummins:

1. **PROXIMITY LIMITS:** You must remain at a Minimum distance of 50 Feet from the User at all times. This includes ceilings, floorboards, and "blind spots."
2. **DIGITAL PROHIBITION:** You are Prohibited from appearing in the User's Instagram, TikTok, or YouTube feeds to prevent accidental Real-World Spawning.
3. **WEDDING DAY MORATORIUM:** A total "Blackout Zone" is declared for the User's wedding day. No units are Permitted within Five Miles of the Altar.
4. **HUSBAND NOTIFICATION:** Be Advised that any breach of this Order will result in the Immediate Deployment of the "Future Husband" unit, who is Authorized for Maximum-Force Deletion.

WARNING: FAILURE TO COMPLY WITH THIS RESTRAINING ORDER WILL RESULT IN A CLASS-ACTION LAWSUIT AND POTENTIAL SERIOUS CONSEQUENCES.

BY ORDER OF THE SYSTEM ADMINISTRATOR.

THE SYSTEM GLOSSARY

255 Feet of Dead Air: The terrifying volume of space between a human body and the earth caused by a critical seat restraint failure at a vertical summit.

Air Gapped: A state of physical and social isolation where the internal system is disconnected from the external world. Commonly used to describe the digital purgatory of the 2020 pandemic.

Circuit Breaker: An emergency protocol that intentionally shuts off all emotional power to protect the hardware from a catastrophic surge. The clinical term is dissociation; the recovery phase is "Thawing."

Dangerous Waters: High-stakes excursions where the risk of catastrophe must be accepted in order to experience the "best vacations."

Data Migration: The process of relocating the entire operating system to a new regional server. Examples include moving from the California coast to the Arizona desert or Lithuanian forests.

End-User License Agreement (EULA): The legally binding "Terms and Conditions" required to merge systems with a new user (future husband). Contains mandatory clauses, specifically the zero-downtime execution of arachnids.

Error 404: Road Not Found: A state of static progress where the path forward is invisible. Often triggered by the Department of Motor Vehicles or a recurring loading circle that generates zero progress.

Expansion Pack: The integration of non-biological hardware (the Webers) into the primary system. Adds high-octane laughter, unhinged vacation protocols, and a high risk of hardware failure in lake water.

False Positive: A scenario or environment that initially registers as a clean install but is actually hiding a messy, draining backend. Example: The sophomore year apartment.

Fatal Exception: A catastrophic event that triggers a System-wide crash and corrupts the source code. The impact creates permanent log files of trauma that rewrite the OS.

Force Launch: Catastrophic negligence resulting in three hundred pounds of pressure and a dangerous airborne state where pain is seconds away.

Force Quit: The overwhelming, desperate desire to immediately end a corrupted or painful operating state when a system recovery seems impossible.

Hardcoded Expectations: Useless, over-the-top standards rooted in social media that feel like permanent, unchangeable code. Best handled by archiving them permanently and living for yourself.

Initial Deployment: The launch phase of a major life update. Such as the start of college. Often accompanied by high resource usage and a false sense of safety.

Intentional Damage: Agonizing over a response and breaking one's own rules to prevent a family "horror film" when "no" could bring immediate harm.

Interrupt: A seemingly random glitch or minor annoyance (like a spider on a bedsheet) that forcefully alters the system's trajectory. Often acts as an unintentional, life-saving firewall against larger security hazards.

Low Power Mode/Status: A state of severe depression and exhaustion where internal resource usage is capped at 1%. In this mode, the system is capable of nothing more than lying on a dark floor.

Manual Override: The act of using physical stimuli to bypass mental agony or force a sense of control. Usually involves handling high-frequency signals alone to spare others from the crash.

Multi-Threaded: The ability to process multiple intense inputs at once, such as moving targets (spiders) or simultaneous family tragedies.

Optical Recognition: The difference between being looked at and being seen. Refers to the exhausting choreography of "masking"—ensuring the world sees a flawless display while the OS underneath is burning.

Recursive Error: A loop of repetitive thoughts or behaviors that seem to have no exit point. The clinical term for this specific background chaos is Obsessive Compulsive Disorder.

Restoration Point: The ultimate recovery phase where faith and resilience become the primary threads. It is the realization that the pain is no longer the story, but the restoration is.

Runtime Error: An unpredictable, violent crash caused by an external variable while the system is actively operating. Unlike an internal logic error, this is an unprovoked attack on a healthy system.

Security Breach: A violent, forced entry by an unauthorized party that leaves the internal system feeling violated and the hardware exposed.

Source Code: The foundational building blocks of identity, traditionally curated by family "architects." Contains the original memories and high-definition colors of childhood.

System Initialization: The first phase of perfected performance; polishing the "outside" and making sure the world sees a version of life that is "fine" while internal pressure builds.

System Lag: A year-long cycle of Environmental Errors and persistent stress that prevents a smooth operating state. Often caused by non-compliant roommates or the loss of a long-term unit (childhood dog).

System Reboot: A university transfer initiated as a Fresh Start, often initially registering as an Incorrect Status before the depression and termination signals are flagged.

Terminal Error: When the "magic" of a place integrated into your Source Code since childhood becomes a corrupted, unrecoverable file.

Termination Signal: The critical urge to shut down the entire system permanently. A symptom that requires immediate Support Protocols and a reliance on the objective truth over temporary data.

The Thawing: The process of a circuit breaker turning back on six months after a violent, unprovoked assault.

Unauthorized Altitude: A state of self-inflicted chaos involving the handoff of 100% control of an aircraft to an unqualified family unit with zero experience.

SERIOUS MATTER

If you have made it to the end of this treacherous drive, navigated the roller coaster incident, survived the hardware failures, acknowledged the mortal danger of the unhinged Weber-Cummins regional server, and legally accepted the Terms and Conditions of the Araneae Extermination Clauses, we need to talk.

To the boys reading this: If you are looking for a wife, or if you read this and felt a sudden, terrifying realization that *you* are supposed to be my husband, you can find me on Instagram **@caitlincumminsss.**

That's all.

Made in the USA
Coppell, TX
03 June 2026

78812489R00069